P9-DDF-366

Carol Stream Public Library
616 Hiawatha Drive
Carol Stream, Illinois 60188

Helpful Ladybugs

by Molly Smith

Consultant: Brian V. Brown
Curator, Entomology Section
Natural History Museum of Los Angeles County

BEARPORT
PUBLISHING

NEW YORK, NEW YORK

Credits

Cover, © Milos Luzanin/Shutterstock; 4T, © Jef Meul/FOTO NATURA/Minden Pictures; 4C, © David Cappaert, Michigan State University, Bugwood.org; 4B, © Yaroslav/Shutterstock; 5, © Jean Michel Labat/Ardea; 7, © Khoroshunova Olga/Shutterstock; 8, © Kim Taylor/npl/Minden Pictures; 9, © Stephen Dalton/Minden Pictures; 10T, © Stefan Sollfors/Alamy; 10C, © Mike Briner/Alamy; 10B, © Cre8tive Studios/Alamy; 11, © Jef Meul/FOTO NATURA/Minden Pictures; 12, © age fotostock/SuperStock; 13, © Jack Clark/Animals Animals-Earth Scenes; 14T, © Runk/Schoenberger/Alamy; 14B, © Patti Murray/Animals Animals-Earth Scenes; 15, © O.S.F./Animals Animals-Earth Scenes; 16T, © Dwight Kuhn/Dwight Kuhn Photography; 16B, © Hans Pfletschinger/Science Faction/Getty Images; 17, © Dwight Kuhn/Dwight Kuhn Photography; 18, © George Grall/National Geographic/Getty Images; 19, © Chris Schuster; 20-21, © Steve Hopkin/Taxi/Getty Images; 22TL, © M. & C. Photography/Peter Arnold; 22TR, © Mitsuhiko Imamori/Minden Pictures; 22BL, © Nigel Cattlin/Holt Studios International Ltd/Alamy; 22BR, © Martin Shields/Alamy; 23TL, © Jim Wehtje/Photodisc Green/Getty Images; 23TR, © Khoroshunova Olga/Shutterstock; 23BL, © O.S.F./Animals Animals-Earth Scenes; 23BR, © Hans Pfletschinger/Science Faction/Getty Images.

Publisher: Kenn Goin
Editorial Director: Adam Siegel
Creative Director: Spencer Brinker
Design: Dawn Beard Creative
Photo Researcher: Beth Brenzel

Library of Congress Cataloging-in-Publication Data

Smith, Molly, 1974-
 Helpful ladybugs / by Molly Smith.
     p. cm. — (No backbone! The world of invertebrates)
 Includes bibliographical references and index.
 ISBN-13: 978-1-59716-584-6 (library binding)
 ISBN-10: 1-59716-584-0 (library binding)
 1. Ladybugs—Juvenile literature. I. Title.

QL596.C65S65 2008
595.76'9—dc22

                        2007040745

For more information, write to Bearport Publishing Company, Inc., 101 Fifth Avenue, Suite 6R, New York, New York 10003. Printed in the United States of America.

10 9 8 7 6 5 4 3 2 1

Contents

Beautiful Beetles

Ladybugs are **insects** with little round bodies.

They can be red, orange, yellow, or black.

They usually have spots.

Ladybugs belong to a large group of insects called beetles.

These beautiful beetles live almost everywhere in the world.

There are about 5,000 different kinds of ladybugs.

A Ladybug's Body

Like all insects, ladybugs have six legs and two antennas.

Their antennas help them feel and smell things around them.

Their legs have little claws that help them climb up plant stems.

Ladybugs and all other insects have a hard covering called an exoskeleton. An exoskeleton protects the soft inner parts of an insect's body.

antennas

legs

7

Taking Off

Ladybugs have two pairs of wings.

One pair is tough and thick.

It covers and protects a pair that is clear and thin.

When a ladybug flies, its thick wings pop open.

The thin wings then beat quickly to lift the ladybug into the air.

Ladybugs beat their wings about 85 times per second when they fly.

Lots of Spots

Different kinds of ladybugs have different numbers of spots.

Some have more than 20 spots.

Some have no spots at all.

The number of spots on a ladybug can help scientists tell what kind it is.

A ladybug's spots fade as it gets older.

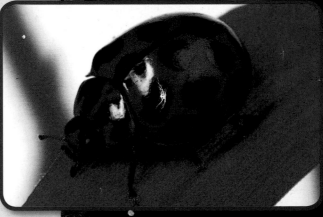

11

Helping Out

Gardeners and farmers like ladybugs because they eat pests called aphids.

Aphids are tiny insects that gather together on plant stems and leaves.

They destroy plants by sucking the juice out of them.

An adult ladybug can eat more than 50 aphids a day.

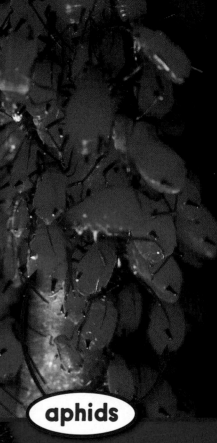

aphids

Some people buy ladybugs for their gardens or farms. Letting ladybugs loose is safer than using poison to kill aphids.

aphid

13

Starting Out

Female ladybugs lay bunches of yellow eggs in spring and early summer.

They lay the eggs on leaves, near groups of aphids.

After a few days, the eggs hatch.

Little creatures with bumpy black bodies come out and start eating the aphids right away.

These baby ladybugs eat as much as they can, and they grow very fast.

A ladybug that has just hatched from its egg is called a **larva**.

eggs

larva

eggs

14

larva

aphid

15

Growing and Changing

As a larva gets bigger, it outgrows its exoskeleton.

The hard covering splits, and the larva crawls out with a fresh, new exoskeleton.

This change—called molting—happens four times.

The larva then changes shape and becomes a **pupa** with a hard outer case.

After a few days, the case splits open, and an adult ladybug comes out.

larva

old exoskeleton

pupa

16

When a ladybug comes out of its pupa case, it has no spots. The spots take a few minutes to appear.

Red Means Stop!

A ladybug's bright colors aren't just pretty.

They are also a warning to enemies, such as birds and spiders. How?

Ladybugs squirt out a smelly yellow liquid when they are in danger.

The liquid makes ladybugs taste terrible to any animals that try to eat them.

The enemies remember the ladybug's bad taste and bright colors, and they do not come back for more!

spider

A ladybug sometimes rolls over and plays dead. This trick fools enemies that don't want to eat dead animals.

Winter Break

A ladybug's life changes when winter comes.

The little insects cannot find aphids to eat, and they cannot fly in cold weather.

So they spend the winter sleeping in trees, under rocks, or even in houses.

When the weather warms up, the ladybugs come out again.

Then they are ready to keep farms and gardens everywhere safe from pests!

Sometimes hundreds or even thousands of ladybugs huddle together during their winter sleep.

21

A World of Invertebrates

An animal that has a skeleton with a **backbone** inside its body is a *vertebrate* (VUR-tuh-brit). Mammals, birds, fish, reptiles, and amphibians are all vertebrates.

An animal that does not have a skeleton with a backbone inside its body is an *invertebrate* (in-VUR-tuh-brit). More than 95 percent of all kinds of animals on Earth are invertebrates.

Some invertebrates, such as insects and spiders, have hard skeletons—called exoskeletons—on the outside of their bodies. Other invertebrates, such as worms and jellyfish, have soft, squishy bodies with no exoskeletons to protect them.

Here are four insects that are closely related to ladybugs. Like all insects, they are invertebrates.

Japanese Beetle

Hercules Beetle

Boll Weevil

Green Tiger Beetle

Glossary

backbone
(BAK-*bohn*)
a group of
connected bones
that run along
the backs of some
animals, such as
dogs, cats, and fish;
also called a spine

insects (IN-sekts)
small animals that
have six legs, three
main body parts,
two antennas, and
a hard covering
called an exoskeleton

larva (LAR-vuh)
a baby ladybug
after it has hatched
from its egg and
before it becomes
a pupa

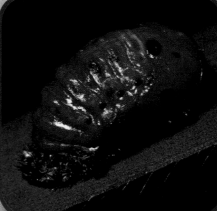

pupa (PYOO-puh)
a ladybug that is
between being a
larva and an adult

Index

Read More

Jango-Cohen, Judith. *Hungry Ladybugs.* Minneapolis, MN: Lerner Publications (2003).

Llewellyn, Claire, and Barrie Watts. *Ladybugs.* Danbury, CT: Franklin Watts (2000).

Learn More Online

To learn more about ladybugs, visit

www.bearportpublishing.com/NoBackbone-Insects

About the Author

Molly Smith has written many nonfiction books and textbooks for children. She lives with her husband and daughter in Norwalk, Connecticut, where she watches ladybugs keep her garden safe.